Prescription to PRISON

PRESCRIPTION TO PRISON

IRVING, KEVAUGHN - PRESCRIPTION TO PRISON

ISBN: 978-1-932448-28-3 (Paperback)
Available in eBook

BUDDLEWRITER

Published By:
BuddleWriter
www.buddlewriter.com

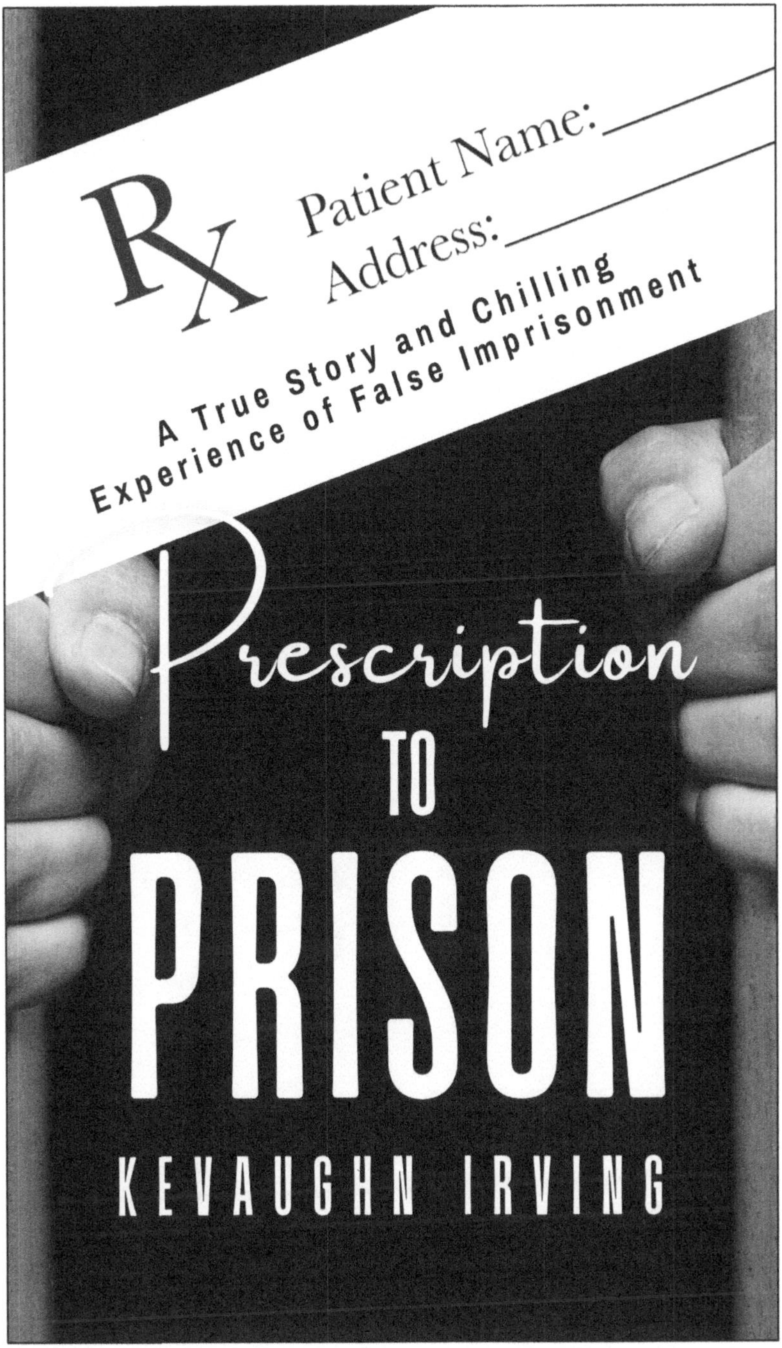
Rx Patient Name:
Address:
A True Story and Chilling Experience of False Imprisonment
Prescription
TO
PRISON
KEVAUGHN IRVING

Foreword

As the attorney who represented Kevaughn Irving from the time of his wrongful conviction through to his successful appeal and vindication at his re-trial, where the court found him not-guilty, I am able to recommend his authentic account of his unfortunate experiences. Kevaughn's sojourn took twelve years and eleven months from the date of his abduction to the affirmation of his innocence by the Supreme Court of Jamaica. After the prosecution witnesses had given their evidence, the court ruling that the evidence produced did not amount to a case against him without even calling upon him to give evidence in his defense.

At the end of the day, the very justice system that initially wrongly accused and condemned him to prison pronounced him not guilty. No system is perfect, but that does not mean that those of us who are the gatekeepers, the administrators of the system, and those who have committed to protect and to serve is relieved from the responsibility to ensure that as far as possible, the system serves the purpose for what it was set up. In this case, the purpose of the system is to secure justice for all.

Very few people who have endured the trauma of false accusations and wrongful imprisonment can re-visit such painful experiences and share them in the public space. For them, this means re-opening of old wounds and re-living the pain. The fact that Kevaughn has taken the bold step of documenting his experience is evidence of his own courage, altruism, and patriotism, including his commitment to an improved justice system.

This documentation of his uphill journey makes interesting reading and should provide useful information for those who have an interest in legal reform or who are simply curious as to how the system works. It is also a cautionary tale for those who become embroiled or are involved in the administration of justice.

Was this a case of genuine error and misunderstanding? Was it the result of a deliberate and malicious concoction, or was Kevaughn simply a target of convenience? Read for yourself and decide. Whatever triggered this dark chapter in this young man's life, the documentation of his experience provides food for thought and enlightenment as to how the system works, its impact on someone who was wrongly accused of a crime, and why we must work together to secure justice for all. Important lessons are to be learned from this shared experience.

Jacqueline Samuels-Brown.

Attorney-At-Law

Dedication

"Who God has blessed, let no man curse."

There are so many people in my life to who I could dedicate this book, but there are two people I want to recognize. My adopted grandmother, **Mrs. Annie Irving**, was one of the most remarkable women in my life. Although she fought a good fight, she lost her battle with cancer. Grandma Irving is no longer around, but I extend my thanks to her.

To **Jorge-Anna Goodwin**, my one and only sister, whom I went to fill the prescription for, and she was only a year old at the time of the incident. My dear sister, if push comes to shove, I would have gone to that pharmacy again to fill the prescription. Anna, as young as you are, I pray that God will bless you with a beautiful life. He is the master of all things, and sometimes in life, we have to have a test to have a testimony. The Lord knows best.

My inspiration came from these two people. I LOVE YOU BOTH!

Table of Contents

Introduction

I am Kevaughn Irving, and it is my most esteemed pleasure to thank you for purchasing my book, ***Prescription to Prison,*** an account of a true-life story I endured. I was inspired to write this book to highlight how unfair the justice system can be in my homeland, Jamaica.

In this book, you will experience some of the daily events at the Tower Street Adult Correctional Center (TSACC) or General Penitentiary, more referred to as GP. It is one of the oldest prisons in Jamaica.

I was framed, yet I never allowed that circumstance or the prison system to break me, as prison life is not a bed of roses. Instead, the ordeal molded me into the person I am today, as I developed solid mental fortitude, which became the foundation of my survival tactic. The motivation from family members and close friends strengthened my resolve to clear my name. There are a lot of innocent inmates who have to be mentally, physically, and emotionally strong not to change while they are incarcerated.

The Lord spared my life throughout my ordeal, and I am eternally grateful to Him. I am a living testimony to the world.

To my readers, even though this is my first book, I hope you are enlightened and uplifted by my tragic story. I was born in the parish of St. Catherine and growing up, I had everything to my comfort. I was never hungry or short of anything. I moved to Kingston with my mother and stepfather, and then we moved back to St. Catherine in 1998. By this time, I was in Grade Six, preparing to sit for the then famous Grade Six Achievement Test (GSAT). I was successful in my examinations and got the opportunity to attend a school of my choice, Charlemont High. Five years later, I successfully passed four subjects in the Caribbean Examinations Council Exams (CXC).

After high school, I studied Level One Livestock Rearing and Level Two Ornamental Horticulture at Ebony Park Heart Academy for one year and six months. I was awarded Trainee of the Month for six months consecutively. Upon graduating from the institution, I also won the Excellent Performance in Early Morning Duties award.

One day, I had an assessment of operating basic farm machinery, which involved the use of a chainsaw. After completing the evaluation, I ventured onto the football field to cut some overgrown trees. When the first tree fell, that gave me a rush of exhilaration, so I moved on to the others. I was now at the third tree, and after cutting the tree, I stepped back to allow the tree to fall; in the process, I realized that I had stepped into a hole. Instantly, I knew something was wrong. I started to fall backward while having the saw in my hands. To regain my balance, I had to let go of the chainsaw handle, leaving my other hand positioned on the throttle. The saw was on full blast as I was falling. There was no way I could have thrown it or tossed it away from myself. The chainsaw blade fell on my knee, ripping through my jeans. It happened in a matter of milliseconds. Miraculously, the jeans jammed the machine. I was ecstatic, shocked, and amazed. I fell to the ground. The hot chain touched my knee, and I knew that it was the mercy of God that had just saved my foot from being chopped off. I sat for about five minutes, trying to gather my thoughts and being thankful for the miracle of not losing a leg. I could not believe what had just occurred. The thought of having one foot made my blood cold. Hours later, while at home, I stared at the considerable cut the chainsaw had made in my jeans. Many thoughts filled my mind, but I thanked God for preventing my foot from chopping off.

A few months passed, and I completed the remaining assessments at Ebony Park. I was ready to start another course in Tractor Operations when one of the instructors approached me and asked if I could assist her by being the demonstrator in that area. I gave it some thought and later accepted the offer. I blossomed in the post and quickly became highly respected at the academy because of my dedication to agriculture, which was my passion. I love animals, and I took pride in doing my job. Unfortunately, my tenure at the institution was temporary as the instructor and I were on unequal terms, so I resigned.

Among the entities I sent job applications was a company where I sought a trainee contractor/supervisor position. A week after applying, I was hired. My duties included various tasks such as overseeing workers and learning to write the payroll. The salary was not much, but it was sufficient to cover immediate needs. I worked six days per week, while I could leave early on some Saturdays. I worked there for a few months until the incident that I could never have fathomed occurred and changed my life forever.

CHAPTER ONE

The Day My Life Changed Forever

Sometimes, I do wish there was a crystal ball into the future. If only I had known that morning when I woke up on Saturday, April 7, 2007, that this day would change my life forever. I would have altered my plans for the day. I did the usual Saturday errands to get myself ready, and went to work. I was young and gainfully employed as a trainee sub-contractor at Trade Winds Citrus farms. A job I enjoyed as it aligned with my then future career goals of being an Agricultural Engineer or a Veterinarian. At Charlemont High, they called me Roger Clarke, nicknamed after the deceased Former Minister of Agriculture. One of my goals was to channel my love for animals into operating an agriculture business while assisting farmers within my community.

I enjoyed working at Trade Winds Citrus farms. It provided an opportunity to fulfill my passion while saving funds to cover tuition expenses to enroll at the College of Agriculture, Science, and Education in Portland. Located in the Bog Walk District, Trade Winds is one of the leading suppliers of juices, with more than 300 acres of land farming mainly a variety of oranges harvested for juices or export. As a Trainee Contractor on the farm, my duties included supervising fifteen to twenty employees daily.

That Saturday, I left work at 3:00 p.m. I made a few stops before heading home. First, I purchased a phone for my mother, then met up with my brother. Lastly, I did grocery shopping for the household.

When I got home, I saw my baby little sister crying. Mother had just got back from the doctor with her. My sister had an inflammation in her right eye causing her much discomfort. Mom gave me the prescription from the doctor and told me to get it immediately filled at the pharmacy.

I went to a pharmacy in Linstead, but the medication was unavailable there. I decided to go to Bog Walk, the next nearest town, to get the drugs prescribed for my sister. While en route, the taxi driver announced that he would not be going to Bog Walk but instead to Spanish Town.

It was about 7:00 p.m. when I got to the pharmacy at Angel's Plaza in Spanish Town to fill the prescription for the eye drop. While inside the pharmacy, my phone rang. It was my mother, checking if I got the medication. I told her, yes, and she instructed me to purchase an item at the nearby supermarket, which I did. Shortly after 8:00 p.m. I made a phone call to my mother, informing her that I was trying to get home but had difficulty getting a taxi.

A vehicle stopped by me, and the driver asked me if I was headed to Linstead. It was a 'robot' taxi. I boarded the beige car; it was nice on the inside with clean seats.

The vehicle drove off with four of us - all men. I was seated on the back passenger side and the man next to me, directly behind the driver, wore dark shades. We drove in silence. These were young men who did not look like criminals, felons, or people who would cause harm. I felt at ease stepping into the vehicle.

Minutes into the journey, I noticed the windows rolling up, yet it wasn't raining. I thought the driver's odd to want the windows to be wound up. That is when I became suspicious. Then it happened. All the comfort of the journey suddenly turned into a nightmare.

The man seated beside me told me to place my hands on the back of the seat in front of me. My heart raced, and instinctively, I turned my head to face him, and that was when I met his stoned face with piercing eyes. I did what he asked me to do.

The other men in the car began to play out their roles, shouting dangerous instructions and treats with expletives at me. One of them pointed a gun at me and told me I should not try anything stupid or they would kill me.

Among the instructions which were coming rapidly, was for me to empty my pockets and hand over cash, phone, and bank cards. I did as told.

The men took my cell phone, mother's bank card, the prescription, and sister's health card. One of the men then threw back the health card and medication at me, mumbling that it was of no use to them.

An interrogation ensued. Question after question, they drove at me. Demanding that I answer truthfully, or else they will hunt down my family. Where did I live? What kind of work did I do? How much money was on the bank card? I answered the questions but told them I didn't know precisely how much was in the bank account for the card as it wasn't mine. Seemingly unsatisfied with my answers, they turned their faces away from me, hissing their teeth and again mumbling.

I, too, turned away from them. That was when I noticed that we were reaching the Bog Walk roundabout. The driver detoured, then stopped to ask someone in the street for directions to the nearest ATM. I wanted to cry out for help, but the man beside me nudged me to sit still. They got the answer, but the man in the passenger seat informed them that there was a police station nearby, so the driver spun the car around. The sudden spin of the vehicle made me even more frightened. I was scared and frantic about the uncertainties that these men would do to me.

I was abducted. Held against my will, I could not think properly; worry and fear began consuming me. I was being transported without consent and against my will, to where I had no idea. I prayed to God to spare me and to send an angel, someone, anyone, to get me out of the car.

Upon reaching a section of the roadway, I looked through the window and saw a young woman signaling the car to stop. The driver drove past her and then stopped the car. The woman walked up to the vehicle. She was probably shorter than me, fat, and it looked like she was wearing a short skirt. I will never know why she chose this car because most women in Jamaica would never get into a taxi at night with four men inside. Seeing her, the driver wound down the window. The driver proceeded to ask her where she was heading. *"Ochi Rios,"* she replied. The driver, a slim dark-skinned man who appeared young, said okay and she boarded. He looked through the rearview mirror and I saw his eyes, but could not read his intentions.

The man sitting beside me pulled me over towards him, pressing the gun to my side. The woman sat beside me unaware of what was happening. The car drove off and the windows went back up.

Instantly, the man in the front passenger seat pulled out his gun, turned to face us, and pointed his gun at the girl. He asked her again where she was headed. He took a cell phone from her, then her purse, and asked her if she had a bank card. She replied, saying no. The man continued questioning her: How old was she? Did she have any children? When was the last time she had sex? She replied by saying she was 26 years old, had one son, and that she had sex the night before. Strangely, she also told them her name.

The men went ahead and did the unimaginable. They assaulted the girl right there in front of me. They touched her in places no real man would touch a woman without consent. I am a Christian and knew how unspeakable and evil these acts were. I felt helpless, not knowing what to do, and completely distraught.

The driver reached back with his left arm and pushed his hand under her skirt, and asked her why she wasn't wearing any underwear. Frantically, she told him that she was allergic to underwear, so she preferred to go without. Mumbling, the driver made another detour, this time heading to the Treadways District, searching, it seemed, for somewhere private to park the car.

After not finding a suitable location, he made a U-turn and headed back to the main road. He then made another turn-off the main road, this time we were now in the vicinity of the Bauxite Plant. He drove onto a private road and ordered us out of the car. Nervously, I struggled to move, not knowing which way to exit.

The man in the front passenger seat came out and opened the door. He pulled the girl out of the car and the other man pulled me out of the car and had the gun pointed at me. The area was pitch black to the point that I could only see the stars and a few lights in the distance from an adjoining community, but I knew I was in the presence of evil.

Two of the men, the driver, and the one in the front passenger seat, yanked the woman some distance away while the other man stood in front of me with the gun pointed at me. While I stood there, he was jeering me to run. He wanted me to make a run of it so he could shoot me dead. The community seemed very empty and lonely. I was not familiar with the area. I was afraid to try anything. I was afraid to try anything. I was indeed scared to run from bullets aiming at me.

When the other two men returned with the woman, the other who had the gun pointed at me gave his friend the gun and then took the woman behind the bushes. A few minutes later, he returned and ordered us back into the car, and the vehicle drove off.

Abruptly the car stopped. The driver ordered the girl out of the vehicle. She began crying and begging them not to kill her. She told them she didn't know where she was. The man in the front passenger seat became furious and got out of the car. He yanked open the door and pulled the woman out. He then threw what looked like some money at her and told her to find her way.

He walked back around the car, got in, and shut the door. The car sped off. I looked at him and saw him roll down the window and throw something through the window, which looked like it may have been something he had taken from the girl.

I was slowly dying inside for fear that these men would surely kill me after what they did to that woman. The driver drove steadily for a bit as if he was searching for something. He then went up to a drive-through ATM. He pulled forward so that I was near the ATM and rolled down the glass, and ordered me to withdraw the money from the card. I tried $15,000 (about US$150) and $10,000 (about US$100), but I was not successful by the grace of God. I tried $5,000 (US$50), and I got the money. The men took the money and the receipt. The driver turned around and looked at me and said, *"Bwoy, u nah go home tonight because we want de rest a de money!"* I was scared because there was a large sum of money on the card. This they knew based on the balance printed on the receipt.

The driver sped off and went back on the main road. I began wondering to myself – would I ever see my family again? How long will they keep me before they release me? Will they withdraw all the money and then kill me? Cold sweat began to wash over my entire body even though air-conditioned was in the car. There were goose pimples on my body, yet my blood ran cold within me.

The vehicle sped up, accelerating to 100mph, a lot of things started running through my mind. I wished I had a knife. I know I would definitely try and escape. I also analyzed what would happen if the police attempted to intercept the vehicle. What would the culprits say? Would they falsely incriminate me? I would be caught in the middle of it all.

By now, we had reached Ocho Rios in St. Ann. I glanced at the clock in the taxi, which said it was some minutes after 11:00 p.m. The driver decided to park at the back of a gas station. There was no one nearby that I could signal to or try to escape. I asked if I could use the bathroom. The driver asked me if I thought they were stupid. I answered no. The man in the front seat came out, opened my door, took me to the front of the car, and said, *"Do yuh ting."* After urinating, I was taken back to the taxi. Upon returning to the vehicle, I saw a tint on the taxi that said *"CRUIZER."*

We sat in the taxi and waited until midnight. The driver then drove to an ATM stand and told me to withdraw the money while one of them stood outside. I tried to withdraw the money, but the machine was defective. I came out and told him the machine was giving me problems. I was taken back to the taxi, and the driver drove to another ATM. I went in to withdraw the money and got it this time.

I considered locking myself inside the ATM, but then, I was not aware whether or not the glass around the ATM was bulletproof. I decided not to take any chances; I withdrew the money and went outside to return to the taxi. The driver took the money from me and asked if I could get any more from the ATM. I told him no. The driver then took us to a drive-through ATM. I was told to try the card again. I could not get any more money because I had reached the withdrawal limit for the day.

The driver then drove the car to a very dark and lonely area. There were no streetlights or nearby houses. The driver stopped the vehicle, switched off the engine and lights, and said, *"Biggs a kill we fi kill yuh cause yuh done see we face already."* My heart raced because I knew I would die when I heard that. That was when the man in the front passenger seat said, *"The only reason we nah kill you is because yuh co-operate and give we de money."* He got out and opened the door on my side and said, *"Run p****."*

I moved so quickly that it seemed to happen in one motion. My feet hit the ground running. That was the fastest I got out of a vehicle. That was the fastest I ever ran. I took off with the hope that I would disappear into the night. I ran past the market and I reached another gas station. I wanted to leave the area so badly. I was worried that the men might think I would go to the police station and come back to kill me. Scared and unsure if I could trust another taxi driver, I went in a red plate taxi and asked the driver where he was headed. He told me, St. Ann's Bay. He asked me where I was going, so I told him to the nearest hospital. He proceeded to ask if I was sick or visiting someone.

I told him about my ordeal. He advised me that I should go to the nearest police station. He took me to the St. Ann's Bay police station. At the station, I reported the incident to an officer. I was told to sit and wait as someone would take my statement. A few minutes later, I asked for a phone call to notify my family about what had happened. I asked for someone to come and pick me up. About half an hour later, the officer returned and took my statement. Sometime after 3:00 a.m., my father arrived, and we headed home—everyone was relieved to see me alive.

About 7:00 a.m., I received a call from the inspector in St. Ann's Bay informing me that they had intercepted the car based on my description. I breathed a sigh of relief. He then proceeded to say, *"The police and the men had a shootout, but the men managed to escape."*

My aunt, who lived in another parish, came to visit me, and everyone was so happy to see that I was alive. Monday morning, I went to the Linstead Police Station to report that I was found since my family had reported me missing. An officer at the Station advised me to make a report at the Spanish Town Police Station because I boarded the vehicle at Angel's Plaza in Spanish Town. That was before I crossed the flat bridge, thus would be out of the jurisdiction of the Linstead Police.

My father drove me to Spanish Town Police Station. I went in, and a female officer started writing the statement. After writing about one paragraph, she stopped and told me to have a seat. I waited until the officer returned to finish taking my statement.

About two hours later, I was surprised to see the young lady who the men sexually assaulted. She stopped, staring at me for about ten seconds, and then the officer took her into another room. Another officer came out and took my statement, which took another two hours. When the policewoman finished, my statement was ten pages long. I had to sign each of the pages, and then I was free to go. They said they would call me if they had any further questions.

CHAPTER TWO

Not So Fast!

After the incident, I returned to work the following Tuesday. I told everyone about the incident. My coworkers were grateful that I was not seriously hurt. At around 4:30 p.m., I received a phone call from the police saying they had a few questions for me and that I should come to the Spanish Town police station. I called my father, asking him to accompany me. He picked me up, and then he picked up my mother at her workplace. When we reached the police station, we were told to wait. After waiting for about two hours, my mother became impatient and informed the officers that we wanted to leave.

It was then that the investigating officer came in and said I would be taken into custody. *"What?"* I said.

The officer repeated herself more clearly, *"You will be taken into custody on suspicion of rape and robbery."*

"What did I do?" I asked as I looked her in the eyes. She told me again that I would be taken into custody on suspicion of rape and robbery. I was in shock and disbelief. She further stated that the young woman in the taxi reported that I robbed and raped her. I was appalled and speechless. My parents were angry and felt helpless. We were all defenseless as the officer took me around to the back of the station and placed me in an empty cell. That night, I could not sleep; I could not believe what was happening to me.

April 10, 2007

The following morning, another officer informed me that they were putting me around the back with the other jailers. My jaws dropped, and my heart came to my mouth. The thought of mixing with criminals made me scared sick. But I did not want to look like a baby because I was honestly afraid, so I held a firm composure. Inside the jail, I was questioned by the other prisoners. I told them my situation, and they said my case was a *"simple buss off,"* meaning I should be freed quickly.

The following day, a man met me at the jail and introduced himself as the attorney appointed to represent me. He said my parents had acquired his services, and he was going to do everything in his power to get me out as soon as possible.

On Sunday, April 15, 2007, I had a question-and-answer session. My lawyer was present, and the officers began to ask questions regarding the incident that had taken place. I spent eight days in lockup before my first court appearance. In court, I was charged with rape, robbery, kidnapping, illegal possession of a firearm, and indecent assault. In addition, I was charged for the other men plus another man that the woman alleged was in the taxi too. In all, I was charged with a total of twenty-five counts. I could hardly believe this was happening as the charges were read against me.

Back in the jailhouse, there were several men with different charges such as murder, shooting with intent, and others. I listened to these men as they shared their ordeal; it seemed like another man was locked up every day. The following morning, I went to court and received $150,000 bail. My lawyer asked for the matter to be transferred to the Gun Court in downtown Kingston. The judge agreed to the request.

Sirens blared as I was driven back to the Spanish Town lock-up. Approximately twenty-five of us were in the truck, accompanied by a police car escorting us to our destination. On arrival, I had to wait for the papers for my release. I had to hand in my passport, and a stop order was placed on my travel documents. I was released on bail. When I got home that evening, all I really wanted was a shower. The shower area at the jailhouse was filthy and fetid.

After my shower, I told my mother, father, and brothers about my days in jail. They listened attentively to the situations I encountered. Although I wasn't free of the charges, it felt good to be home with my family in a familiar space.

CHAPTER THREE

She Said ...

In her statement, the woman said she had known me since 2003. She stated that I made regular visits to her bar in Bog Walk, St. Catherine. Utter astonishment – that was a lie. As I stated before, I am a Christian. I do not go to bars, and I do not drink. She also said during that particular time frame when the incident occurred; I was also working in the Bog Walk area.

On that particular night, she said she stopped a car at the Bog Walk round-a-bout, and only the driver was in the vehicle, so she opened the back door and went in the car. After crossing the traffic light, she claimed the car had stopped, and four men approached the vehicle.

Telling her story, she said she tried to leave the car, but the driver pulled a gun on her. She said he had a 45 with an extended clip. The woman also said that all five men raped her and forced her to perform oral sex on them; she also said all five men ejaculated within her. In her statement, the woman said I was the last one who raped her. I forced her to perform oral sex on me, and that she grabbed my balls and squeezed them so hard that I cried out. She said the other four men pulled their guns and pointed them in her face. She said she told them if they shot her, I would die too because she would not stop squeezing my balls. After all of that, she said I went behind her, made one jolt, and came inside her. Before the men raped her, she also said that I directed the men to somewhere; and upon seeing that the area was populated, the men took the gun from me, hit me in the neck, and asked me if I took them for idiots.

Finally, the woman said she went in the taxi initially because she had driven in that vehicle on previous occasions. Upon entering the car, she realized that it was a different driver. It was also stated that the police wanted to find out who the car owner was in question and completed an investigation on the ordeal.

CHAPTER FOUR

At The Trial

I went to court on numerous occasions before a trial date was finally set for April 1, 2008. During the trial, the young lady and I testified as to what transpired that night. At one point, she told the court that only she, God, and I knew what took place that night. I presented the court with the prescription and the bank receipts to aid my statement. All I could do was share the truth and the evidence supporting that I did not commit these crimes. I was an innocent man, falsely accused, and more importantly, I was also a victim of this crime spree led by those three men on Saturday, April 7, 2007.

The trial continued until it was now time for the closing statements. It was no coincidence. God began to show up and show out in my favour on that day. Surprisingly, the prosecutor told the court that she identified inconsistencies in the woman's statement during the closing arguments. The prosecutor said she had doubts about the woman's story.

The prosecutor brought her statement to a close and took a seat. My lawyer then gave his closing statement. He vigorously reaffirmed my innocence, and he, too, pointed out inconsistencies in the victim's testimony that supported the prosecutor's statement. As a result, my bail was extended, and I went home that day, thanking God, but I knew that I still had a significant fight to come.

CHAPTER FIVE

A Second Chance To Tell About My Ordeal

(The following were letters written to my attorney by my aunt, Mom, and Neighbour)

My Aunt Carolyn also testified on my behalf:

On April 7, 2007, at approximately 9:00 PM, I received a call from my sister, Maxine, who said she had sent my nephew to the pharmacy and he had not returned. She was concerned as the sojourn was expected to take maximum of an hour, and it was unusual for him not to return home promptly after an errand. Maxine said she spoke to him while he was in Spanish Town (Angel's Plaza) after completing the purchase and instructed him not to go into Spanish Town but instead take a taxi home.

Shortly after, she called his phone, but she received no response. She was particularly concerned because at first, it seemed as if the phone line was open, and she could hear noises but did not get him on the phone. Later, all subsequent calls went to the 'voicemail.' Furthermore, I started dialing his number and did not get a response. Knowing my nephew to be a child who spent most of his time at home on computer games, I became worried. It was clear that something was wrong as someone always knew where he was at any particular time. Based on what was happening in the country and in that part of the Spanish Town area, I was concerned. I called up a few friends, and we started praying for his safe return. The worrying, praying, and calling to his phone continued until the early hours of the morning. I could not sleep. Before daybreak, the following morning, my sister called me and said that he was found and that his father was on the way to the St. Ann's Bay Police Station to pick him up. Based on the threats he had received, she said she was cautious not to say much on the telephone. Later that morning, my family and I journeyed from Mandeville to Linstead to see my nephew. We were joyous and thankful that he was alive.

He told us of his ordeal. He expressed how he felt at each stage. He told us what actions he considered taking but was afraid to do it. Although he was exhausted and physically drained from his ordeal, he repeatedly recounted the incident to family members and close friends. Each sequence of events was consistent at every point. While I was in his presence in Linstead, he received a call from an Inspector assigned to the St. Ann's Bay Police Station.

Kevaughn willingly supplied all information intending to assist the police in catching the criminals. He told us that the Inspector said he should rest and go to the Linstead Police Station the next day. On Tuesday, April 10, 2007, my sister informed me that a police officer had called Kevaughn and told him to report to the police station to give further information. While there, he was taken into custody for suspicion of being a participant in the same incident he had reported being a victim.

I was with a group of professionals to whom I had related my nephew's traumatic situation. I told them what was happening and that he had been arrested and charged for the crimes of which he was a victim. They advised me to get an attorney immediately. Some names were suggested and a lawyer was retained. I could not imagine my nephew spending the night in jail. I asked the lawyer that same night, and he explained what had happened. He promised to see my nephew the next day. I made arrangements with the lawyer for my sister to meet with him. My sister had just started a new job on the night of my nephew's arrest. She asked his father to meet with him to pay a deposit for retaining the lawyer's services.

The lawyer informed me that it was best for me to contact get through to him at night because, during the day, his cellular phone was often off. He went to see Kevaughn as agreed. His reaction afterward to me was encouraging. *"I see that the boy is innocent. I have spoken to him, and if you take one look at him, you know that he could not hurt a fly"*. He also said that he doubted that my nephew had ever had sexual intercourse in his opinion.

I discussed with the lawyer all pertinent information relating to my nephew, including but not limited to:

1. The type of child my nephew is: Responsible, honest (his mother entrusted him with her bank card, giving him all access to her savings without fear and not on the night of the incident only), hardworking, pleasant, and polite
2. The sequence of events that night, including calls made between Kevaughn and his mother, and the time at which the calls were made.
3. The fact that in our possessions were the receipt from the pharmacy and the prescription and drugs purchased.
4. It could be established that my nephew was a productive member of society. When he graduated from high school, he pursued a programme in agriculture at the Ebony Park Heart Academy in

Clarendon. He was very devoted to his studies and utterly engrossed in the projects at the school.

5. His love for agriculture, which, in addition to his complexion and size, earned him the nickname Roger Clarke after the late Minister of Agriculture.
6. Several people were more than willing to stand as character witnesses on my nephew's behalf. Individuals include senior police officers from his neighbourhood, a person from his previous school, past and present employers, elders at church, and other people in his community.

I must admit that I was naïve to the intricacies of the justice system. I thought that justice would prevail with the young man's truthful testimony and what I felt was a highly recommended and respected attorney. I attended the first hearing at the Spanish Town courthouse and met the lawyer for the first time. He was very reassuring when I expressed anxiety. He told me not to worry as he would get him out of there. He told me there were apparent inconsistencies in the young lady's statement.

Then situations took a downward turn with the lawyer. My sister could not often get through to the lawyer as he would sometimes not take her call. She would be calling him after visiting my nephew, and he did not take her call, or so she felt. I tried to arrange for my sister to meet with the lawyer at his office to discuss the case and the line of defense he would take. The lawyer, however, did not think it was necessary, so he never arranged for the meeting. He kept saying 'too many people were in his case, and he wants us to leave him alone as he knows what he was doing. Long periods passed without hearing from the lawyer, so we lost confidence in him.

My sister was by now very concerned and informed me that she was advised to take the case to another lawyer because of what seemed to be the lawyer's lack of interest and unacceptable performance. We gave him all the pertinent information, yet his results were less than unsatisfactory. When my sister could not get through to the lawyer, she discussed her concern with me, and I, in turn, discussed them with him.

The lawyer only called my sister to ensure the agreed sum would be paid on time. During the trial's final days, I related my nephew's situation to another friend who directed me to speak with another attorney. The friend started questioning if investigations were completed on both plaintiff and the defendant. He also wanted to know if character witnesses were called or if the attorney visited my nephew's school? He asked was the DNA requested and tendered into evidence. When it became clear that none of what he was suggesting was undertaken, he was very cautious in his response and said, *"Your attorney is a man of experience. He should know what to do"*.

After the day of the sentencing, the lawyer never called, nor have I spoken with him since. Our nightmare continued when the lawyer started to be rude and abusive to my sister. She reported that he said he was *"annoyed with you people,"* referring to the family. My sister's only reason for calling him was to ask for receipts for the paid sums. At that point, she questioned him about the DNA we kept referring to, he told her he was not aware of it, and he was the person who suggested we get the DNA done.

Now, the person we paid to represent us had turned on us. I felt and still feel very bad as I was the one who recommended that lawyer. I relied on the recommendations of people I trusted; I perceived them to be people of integrity and expected professionalism of the legal fraternity. As civilians, we seek the wisdom of lawyers to be our representatives in the quest for freedom. So, this family engaged the services of a registered and practicing attorney from whom we expected professional assistance, thoroughness in preparation, and a passion for and commitment to upholding justice.

LETTER FROM NEIGHBOUR:

To Whom It May Concern:

I am a concerned parent, a resident of Linstead in the Parish of St. Catherine. I have known Kevaughn Irving for ten years. He attended the same primary and high schools as my children. I have known this young man to be quiet, jovial, mannerable, law-abiding, intelligent, and humble. Hearing the sad situation of him being accused of these offenses, I am still shocked. I am unable to eat; thus, losing weight when I consider it could be my son in this unfortunate position who is now in college and has to travel daily.

His co-workers, friends, greatly miss Kevaughn Irving and his younger sister, whom he went for to purchase medication when this situation occurred. I pray day and night that the judge of the court will find it in their heart to think about "what if it was their child that was being accused and taken from the society innocently."

God knows that Kevaughn is innocent and is a victim, just as the young lady who claimed he raped her.

CHAPTER SIX

My Verdict

Ironically, the day I received my verdict was precisely a year to the date I was locked up. It was now April 9, 2008, and my whole life had taken a dramatic turn. I had been very uncomfortable throughout the entire ordeal. It is a terrifying experience to be abducted and robbed, but it is emotionally horrifying to be framed for such a hideous crime by someone. I went into depression. I had changed jobs since being out on bail. I went to work that day but was uneasy because I knew it was the day I would receive my verdict. I was positive about my innocence but had doubts about the justice system. I had mixed emotions.

My parents picked me up about noon, and we proceeded to the courthouse. The matter was set for 2:00 p.m. We were early, so we waited. About 15 minutes before 2:00 p.m., they called my name, and I entered the courtroom. My parents had to wait outside because Jamaica's judicial system states that unless you have a matter before the court, you are not allowed inside the courtroom

The court was called to order, and the judge reviewed my case. She started the trial with a surprise statement. She told me that she was refusing all the evidence submitted on my behalf. The judge said she was giving the woman the benefit of the doubt. The judge found me guilty on all five charges. My heart skipped a beat as she spoke. I began wondering if all this was real. I also asked what had happened to the DNA evidence? The police had taken it from me, and I knew this alone was enough to set me free.

I was so shocked I could not speak. The case was adjourned. I was handcuffed and taken to the 'bullpen' (courthouse jail). On the way to the 'bullpen,' I saw my parents. My father's face was filled with anger. My mother cried as she saw me in the handcuffs. I calmly told to her not to cry — *"I will be okay. You have to be strong for everyone,"* I told her. Although I felt like my life was now headed downhill, I had to be strong for my family; but on the inside, a small voice was telling me… it was over.

CHAPTER SEVEN

Held

I spent approximately one month at the Kingston Central lockup. The cell was a large block, and four of us lived together. I was given three meals a day and allowed snacks from family members. We were allowed to have a home-cooked meal on Sundays, and we were permitted to see family members. Visitors could give us snacks such as bun, banana chips, and soda.

Life in jail is rough. You have no freedom whatsoever. You are confined to one area. I was only allowed to leave the cell when I wanted to shower or use the toilet. Each cell is allowed 20 minutes to use the bathroom. There were also people from feuding gangs, so the officers took caution during the allotted bathroom break. We only received half of a toothbrush, as jailers would break the brush, and the handle part would be sharpened as a weapon. The scent in the jail was also awful. It was a mixture of sweat, poor septic practices, and faeces. The walls were dirty and filled with stains; rats and roaches lived in every crevice of this space.

In all honesty, I was petrified! I could not act soft or expect to be treated like a baby, but I knew I had to be strong mentally for my friends and family members. After a month, I would be transferred to the General Penitentiary. It was now a matter of days since I had been imprisoned. It was hell having to sleep on the makeshift board bed and inhaling septic air that reeked of faeces night after night. On one visiting day, I was anxious about the regular visit from my parents. However, when my father arrived, he told me that my grandmother had passed. I was heartbroken. She had been battling cancer for some time, and the news of me being locked up was just too unbearable for her. She died in her sleep. My father said she gave up her battle and let go once she heard the news about me being convicted. My family kept this from her until my uncle mistakenly mentioned it to her, thinking she knew.

The death of my grandmother shook me to the core. I could hardly eat that day. I wanted to cry, but no tears came. It was the worst possible news that I could possibly have gotten. I began to wish that I had never existed. I asked my father if he could call my girlfriend and ask her to represent me at the funeral as I was unsure if I would even be able to make it there. Later, I was shocked when he told me that she did not attend the funeral. She never visited me, not once while I was incarcerated.

A few days later, a man visited me and told me he was my Probation Officer. He questioned me and said that he went to my community and interviewed several people, including family members, and the responses were impressive. He assured me that he would do what he could to assist with my case.

CHAPTER EIGHT

Sentencing: May 9, 2008

It was a big day for me. I would be taken to court for sentencing. I got up at 5:00 a.m. and got ready. The names of each inmate were called, and we were huddled into a van, two-by-two, in handcuffs. There were twenty of us in the vehicle, seventeen prisoners, the driver, and two other officers, while a police jeep followed. I was the only prisoner who was not in handcuffs. The journey to the courthouse was about five minutes. As we reached our destination, we were searched and placed in the bullpen. An officer approached me and told me that my hearing was at 2:00 p.m.

The cell I was placed in had approximately twenty-five men inside, and the place was sweltering. I sat and waited for about two hours. I was so nervous all this time, not knowing what to expect. I started asking myself, *"Why was I here in the first place? What did I do to deserve this? Why me?"* A female officer came and called my name along with two others. I was again cuffed and escorted to the courtroom. Arriving in the room, I realized that my lawyer was not present. I began to worry. Shortly after I arrived in the courtroom, a woman approached me and asked my name. I told her, and she said she would be my representative. I felt relieved but shocked as to why my lawyer was not present. The judge walked in about five minutes later, and the court was called to order. It felt like a cloud of darkness had entered the room when she came in, but I knew God was with me, so I remained calm. Shortly after my name was called, I stood, and the officer released the handcuffs and escorted me to the box. While in the box, an officer took the stand and read my affidavit. After that, my Probation Officer took the stand and gave the court his findings on me. He told the court that background checks revealed I was a hardworking individual, and this was my first run-in with the law. He asked the judge to consider giving me a suspended sentence in his closing statement.

When the prosecution read out the charges, the court clerk looked at me shockingly because of the number of charges I was facing. He got up and went to the prosecution and asked her if all these charges were mine. I felt that my heart was literally in my mouth through all of this. Many things were running through my mind, such as, *"What is the judge going to say? Is she going to sentence me or throw out the fraudulent case?"*

After the lawyer representing me spoke, the judge seemed impressed with my background that at one point, she even smiled. When I saw the smile on her face, I felt as though a load had been lifted off my head.

CHAPTER NINE

First Judge's Decision

Silence filled the courtroom. Then the judge spoke – breaking the silence. As I stood there, I looked her in the eyes as she spoke. She looked back at me and said she had thought long and hard about what sentence to give me. She told me that she was impressed with my background and that it's hard these days to find a young man in my age group who had not been entangled with the law. She further stated that I'm not a threat to society or even my community, but she could not give me a suspended sentence due to the seriousness of my charges. That's when it dropped on me like a bomb. I WAS GOING TO PRISON! It felt like someone had just stabbed me in the back with a dagger. Instantly, my world turned upside down. As she continued to speak, I held my composure. I listened as she laid down the sentences as follows: rape -5 years; robbery with aggravation -3years; illegal possession of a firearm -5years; abduction - 3years; and indecent assault-3years. She further stated that the charges were to run concurrently. Concurrent means that I would be doing all those years simultaneously, while consecutive is having to complete one sentence before starting the other. I just wanted to leave the courtroom. I wished that I was dreaming. At one point, I even pinched myself to make sure I was not dreaming. My head felt very light, and my knees were weak. After laying down the charges, the judge asked if I had anything to say. I said no.

I was handcuffed and taken from the courtroom. I was taken into a room on my way from the courtroom, and my parents walked in. I began telling my mother what had transpired inside the courtroom. My father was distraught. I did not know if it was the fact that the lawyer had not attended court or the fact that I was going to prison. My mother began to cry. I told her not to and encouraged her to be strong. Shortly after, the lady who represented me explained the sentence and told us concurrently. She told me that I should consider appealing the case. She said that I would be serving a three-year and four-month prison sentence. Moments later, I was told to *"wrap it up."* We said our goodbyes and I was taken back to the bullpen. I held back the tears; I had to be strong for my family and myself. *"Can you imagine going to prison for a crime you did not commit?"* I thought. I wished I could just disappear at that moment.

My life seemingly had taken a route downhill, and it bothered me. I could not sleep. I kept questioning God why He would allow such a horrible thing to happen to me. I was scared. Yet, I came to the determination I just had to live with it for now.

CHAPTER TEN

Transfer to General Penitentiary

I Did not feel like myself on the morning of my transfer to the General Penitentiary, I did not feel like myself. I got up, then shortly after, I took a shower and went back to my cell. On the outside, the sky was overcast; it looked like how I felt. I called the officer and asked him if he could check to see if the papers for my transfer were ready. He left and came back shortly after. He told me they were prepared, but he was unsure when I would be transferred. I knew, though, I could be transferred at any time, once the papers were ready.

I sat down and waited in my cell, listening to the names being called to the people attending court, and that's when I heard my name. I was so shocked because the moment had finally arrived for me to go to prison. I was told to pack up all my belongings and take them with me; I barely had any clothes because I had sent them out with my parents on a previous visit.

I was the last person to be placed inside the van, and to my surprise, I was the only one not handcuffed. I knew it would be senseless to try and escape. That was the last thing on my mind. What mattered most was where I was headed to and the people I would be around from now on. The van was filled to carrying capacity. I now knew what it felt like to be packed like sardines in a vehicle.

The van sped off, and there was also another police car behind escorting the van. It was only a matter of minutes before we arrived at my new home. Upon arriving, the officers inside the van had to leave their firearms with the officers in the car. No weapons were allowed inside the prison, not even police officers were exempted. The van drove in slowly, leaving the escort outside, and the first thing that caught my eye was the prison's motto: **NONE SHALL**

ESCAPE. That sign needed no explanation. There were seven of us transferred from jail to prison that morning. We were taken upstairs to the reception area. The officer had a receipt book, and that is when I realized that an individual is received as a BODY when first entering prison. That means you come in alive, but you might not leave that way. I was searched first and told to declare anything in my possession. Anything I didn't declare would be confiscated. I was then registered, and the rules and regulations of the prison were read to me.

The registration process took about two hours; the warder took my height, background information, fingerprints, and photograph. Before being sent to my new cell, I was given one cup, one bowl, one tissue, and bath soap. I was then escorted to my section. In jail, I was told that I should not go to prison without money if it's even to have a $100. I didn't have any money, but I had God with me. I believed that He would get me through it once God brought me to it. If it weren't for the Mighty One who sits high and looks low, I wouldn't be alive today to tell this story.

The warder in charge of the section called me and began questioning me about my charges. I told him. He instructed another warder to escort us, the new prisoners, to the stores to pick up a mattress. When we came back, supper was being served: brown stewed chicken back and white rice. I collected my meal and went to my cell. For some reason, everyone was questioning me about what I was charged for, how many years my sentence was, and if I had any money on me. The truth was; that I wasn't scared but nervous. I had never before seen that many men in one place.

In the cell where I was placed, I had a choice to sleep on the ground or in a hammock. However, it's a tradition in prison that all new prisoners sleep in a hammock. The hammock was hell. It was a piece of cloth held up by two pieces of board and eight other pieces of rope. The cell was tiny, approximately four by eight feet, and so small that three inmates could not sleep on the floor.

I was a big guy with a robust frame. It is no surprise that my body broke the hammock before my first week in prison ended. I wept. I felt so bad being where I was for something I didn't do. I had to try and make myself comfortable for now, at least, and most importantly, try to keep a sane mind.

CHAPTER ELEVEN

Prison Life

As a child, hearing about prison was a very grim description. I often heard that everyone in prison is homosexual, and they have the tendency to fight a lot. I was also told that they are all murderers, rapists, or robbers. Consequently, that was a place I never wanted to go, not even in my wildest dreams, but not everything in life you wish for that you get.

The Tower Street Adult Correctional Centre, formerly General Penitentiary (GP), was built about 150 years ago. The penitentiary had a holding capacity of approximately 650 to 700 males. The walls made of bricks were about ten feet tall. Its two entrances were later changed to one main entrance and exit. Each cell was made to hold one individual, but drastic changes had to be made due to the high crime rate in Jamaica. Cell doors had to be reinforced with thicker material to be more durable than it was previously. Prisoners are entitled to three visiting days, which includes a food day, in which they can receive a home-cooked meal from families and friends. They aren't allowed to see their family members on food day. They can receive a few pieces of clothing and other personal effects. Prisoners are only entitled to four visits per month. Family members can only talk with the prisoners for about five minutes or sometimes a little more. They are sometimes given the privilege of the family week, where they can hug loved ones and children. That is probably the day most prisoners look forward to, other than the day they receive their freedom.

Life in prison is deplorable. Living conditions are below the living conditions of a human being. Instead of one person in a cell, there are three or sometimes more, depending on the number of prisoners. There are a lot of sections, but the cells are tiny, 4x8 or 5x10 feet. Only two people can sleep on the ground and the other in the hammock.

There is no bathroom in the cell, no toilet. Instead, prisoners have to get a plastic jug, cut a hole in it, and tie a piece of string on it. Each prisoner has one, so they can urinate in it when inside the cell. In the morning, remove them from the cell, empty them in the urinal, wash them out and place them back in the cell. If they wish to defecate, they would have to make it known to other cellmates to go towards the back of the cell. Afterward, they spread a piece of plastic and then newspaper, and when he was finished, he would take it up in a bag and place it outside the cell until in the morning. It was emptied into the garbage; the prisoner then washes out the cell with soap and bleach.

The prison system was very corrupt. A prisoner would dislike you just because you receive a visit from family members. In the morning, prisoners get out of their cells at approximately 9:30, shortly after breakfast is served. Breakfast consisted of tea, bread (this bread was baked at the Spanish Town prison and sent to G.P daily), and sometimes, they might cook callaloo or egg, and once per week, we might get an orange.

At about 11:30 a.m., lunch was served. After this, the prisoners were locked down. Prisoners who work at GP can work throughout the day. The reason for the lockdown is to facilitate the warder's lunchtime. Warders go on lunch from noon until about 1:30 p.m. Warders and fellow prisoners prepare the food. There was a school inside the prison where prisoners who could not read had an opportunity to learn how to. There was also a tailor shop, a welding shop, and a hospital. Even though it had a lot to offer, one thing was for sure...the prison was not a place of rehabilitation. Prisoners have too much time to premeditate. One can only learn if one wants to.

The bathroom area consisted of a shower, two sinks to wash, and two so-called toilets. One toilet was in a pit, and the other toilet was a regular toilet, but there was no way that over 100 men per day could use it, and it remained clean. Not all prisoners who come to prison receive mattresses. So, if they are without family members, they will probably have to spread cardboard on the ground or old clothes. In Jamaica, it was legal for inmates to have a bulb for lighting in the cell. Prison could be described as a bomb waiting to explode. Inmates often fight. We also experienced water shortages in prison.

There are a lot of innocent men in prison, and I found that out during the time of my incarceration. Jamaica's justice system needs to be deeply examined as due to absentee lawyers or financial difficulties; one could be imprisoned. Even a lack of investigation by police personnel has sent several men to GP. Apparently, there is a need for an overhaul of Jamaica's justice system, especially where some appointed lawyers cannot carry out their duties professionally. The investigative skill of some law enforcement officers needs to be improved.

CHAPTER TWELVE

My Prison Journal: A Tragedy

(Daily account of my activities while in G.P.)

Friday, May 16, 2008

I hardly slept the first night in prison, but I made it through the night alive. My cellmates seemed ok so far; although I had no idea as to what their charges were, they seemed ok, I lay in the cell, and all that came to mind was just how good God was, and He will always work something out for His children, He will never give us more than we can bear. That night, for the first time in my life, I saw a strange insect, so I asked my cellmate. He told me it was a chink (bedbug), a blood-sucking insect, that loved warm places, and I guess the scent of the prison was also a huge contribution. I thought about all I was facing and how I would have to adapt to it. I closed my eyes, and before I knew it, it was morning; I was awakened by a warder saying Muster check (a headcount of prisoners). My cellmate answered and said three of us were in the cell. At 9:00 a.m. the signal for unlocking was called shortly after which I saw three warders approaching my section, they unlocked each padlock, and then, one pulled the "brake" (a mechanism used to hold all the cell doors shut). I had to urinate in a bottle because I had nothing else to use. My cellmate told me that I would usually have received a water jug that I would have to be used to urinate at night, empty it in the morning, then wash it out, and place it back in the cell.

There are nearly 100 of us in the section and only one shower, two urinals, and two toilets. There is also a sink used to do any washing that needs to be done. A 1000-gallon of water tank supplies the section, which to my surprise, is empty by half-day, so inmates would have to seek water elsewhere in the prison. I sat in my cell for most of the day, observing the running and reading my Bible. Breakfast was served at about 10:00 AM, and lunch at 11:30. After which, the prison is locked down. The warders go on lunch and return at about 1:00 PM.

When the prison was unlocked, I asked the officer in charge of the section to escort me to the appeals and bail office. He instructed a junior warder to accompany me. Upon arriving, I was told to sit and wait. I was asked a few questions, and I was also made aware of the fact that if I appealed my case, I would not actually be serving a prison sentence. Therefore, my sentence would be suspended pending the outcome of my appeal. That, however, did not matter to me as I was sure of my innocence, and there were a lot of flaws in my case, so I am sure someone would at some point pick up on those errors. I signed a form and was escorted back to my section. It was now suppertime. I collected my supper and went back to my cell. The prison was locked down by 3:00 PM Saturday

May 17, 2008

I woke up this morning intending to go to the church in the prison, so I got up and did what I had to do and had a shower. I then went to my cell to get ready, just then, an orderly approached my cell door. He asked me if I was interested in going to the classes being offered in the prison. I told him yes; he outlined to me what the course was about and wrote my name and cell number down. Prison is like a small community in itself. There is a tailor shop, a church, a barbershop, a hospital, a tuck shop, a school, and a recording studio. By this time, it was time for lunch to be served, so the church-going was now out of the picture. I collected my soup and went back to my cell. Soup is always cooked on a Saturday, my cellmate told me. After the warders came back from lunch, I went to get some water in my jug, because there was no water in the cell. Instead, I prepared for the lockdown which usually occurred about three o'clock. Through all this, a song kept coming back to my head; it's a song I learned in jail:

"I wanna go home on Freedom Street.

I wanna go home to my family

After man a no lumber fe a sleep pan no concrete,

I wanna take my kids to the beach

My girl is struggling for her daily meal

Can't tek the pressure can't tek the heat

I wanna go home to my family."

May 18, 2008

Today started like any other day. I followed the same routine. About lunchtime, the "orderly" on the section approached me and told me to pack my things because I was moving to another cell. I was currently located in number 30 cell. So, the guy in number 7 was placed in my cell, and I was being moved. My heart was racing, I could not understand why I was being moved, but I believed that it was because I was new. I did what I was told and packed my things. The new cell had two of Jamaica's most notorious men.

Just by looking at them, you would be afraid. When I entered the cell, I asked them where I was going to sleep. One said "in the hammock", I was shocked and wondered how the heck was I going to ever fit in that thing. I am new; so fewer questions would be best right now. My cellmate told me I have two ears and one mouth, so that meant I should listen twice as much as I speak. Well, it is now bedtime. I tried to jump up in the hammock, but the pan I stood on was not sturdy enough, so I fell and hit my knee and knocked over a few of the men's stuff. I felt so stupid, but I held my composure. After several attempts, I finally made it. This was my first time in a hammock, and I felt uncomfortable. Imagine being on a piece of cloth tied by eight pieces of string and being about six feet from the ground. That was my bed. My cellmate mumbled how the orderly put men in the cell to kill him. Deep down, I was scared. I was wondering what would happen if the cord burst. I would be injured, but I was also sure my cellmates would be hurt, which I was afraid of happening.

May 19, 2008

Last night was hell. I did not get any sleep because of the hammock, but it was finally morning. My new cellmates seem ok so far, and I respected them as two elders in prison.

I lost my appetite. I can hardly eat anything. Every day, I ask myself what I was doing here. I did not deserve to be here. I had to let it sink in my mind that I was already here, so it was something I was going to have to live with, at least for now. Each day, my cellmates would tell me the do's and don'ts around the prison. That also made it clear to me that when you go to prison, don't be expected to be treated like a baby. I could not believe where I really was, and I wondered to myself why and how someone told such a lie and how the system could be so unfair in sending an innocent man to prison. Just then my cellmates and I had a conversation and he asked me if I knew the definition of rules. He told me that **Rules** *are a system set up for you to get caught.*

May 20, 2008

Last night, I barely slept as I thought the hammock would tear under my weight, but, luckily enough, it did not. I woke up early and tried to get out of the hammock and it tore in two. I began to wonder to myself why I am so slight at times. I started to feel discouraged and depressed. I wondered why I was feeling this way. My first cellmates began to say I treated them badly and even tried to get me in some mix-up. It was there and then I realized that if they weren't friends with you, they would try to make your life a living hell. So, I made sure I avoided them from now on. They even tried to extort things from me at one point, but I stood my ground. You should watch what you are doing in and around the prison or you will end up dead. It is best to look and listen twice as much as you speak.

Today I got a visit from my dad, it was great to see him, although, I could hardly hear what he said to me. But, it was good to see him. He brought me some clothes, money, and deodorant. After lockdown, my cellmates and I chatted then I fell asleep.

May 21, 2008

I woke up feeling refreshed. I didn't sleep in the hammock as one of my cellmates was kind enough to exchange his sponge for the hammock. I woke up to see one of my cellmates staring at me. It was then that I realized my foot was on his sponge, I quickly moved. I was badly in need of a haircut, so I went to the barber, and shortly after I went to my cell. In our society, the prison system is so corrupt. It is better to keep to yourself. Any of you out there coming to prison for the first time, remember 'prison is not a bed of roses', so you'll have to keep your head on your body or you will be disrespected.

There is a rumor in Jamaica that most of the prisoners are gays, which is not so. These prisoners are located on a section to themselves. They have to be secluded from the other prisoners, or they will be killed. We here, in Jamaica, are homophobic, so there are certain cultures we cannot adapt to.

Today was a day we, in prison, called food day: a day, in which, we could receive a home-cooked meal and fruits. I missed home so much that is why I know that there is no place like home, which is so true. On food days, we aren't able to see our families.

May 22, 2008

Today I got up, and I was going to tidy my cell. First, I used a piece of sponge to sweep out the cell, after which, I proceeded to polish the cell using another sponge and then used another piece of cloth. My cell is the cleanest on the whole section. My cellmates warned me that I should be very skeptical about my surroundings. They were very clean too. One major issue I had was that they smoked. But what could I do other than humble myself?

May 23, 2008

Shortly after I woke up this morning, an orderly came and called my name and told me that I should meet at the gate when I finished my chores. He took me to the Chaplin. The Chaplin asked me a few questions and advised me that I could always come and talk to him if I ever needed someone to talk to. Shortly after, I went to the classroom area for a class on entrepreneurship. I had to build the courage to tell my life story. That class was very interesting, and I learned a lot. When I got back from class, it was almost time for lockdown. When I got in my cell, I thought about what I wanted to do with my life from here on out. There are certain goals in my life: long-term, short-term, and medium-term goals.

Short Term Goal:

My short-term goal is to educate myself in any way possible while I am here. To think positively, even when things seem impossible. I would also want to build on my relationship with the Lord.

Medium-Term Goal:

After leaving here, I would like to further my studies in Computer Technology and Agriculture. I would also like to obtain a job in any of the two fields, and work for about 10 years. In this time frame, I hope to buy my house and vehicle. I would also like to get married and get 2-3 kids.

Long Term Goal:

I want to open my own business preferably in the ornamental/horticultural field. I would also like to build a greenhouse and retire at age 60 with my wife and leave the business to the children.

May 25, 2008

Today marks one week and three days being transferred to prison. It has not been bad, but it isn't good either. Who could ever have a good day in prison, but the greatest thing is that I have life? I basically know most of the 'running's' in and around the prison. The safest way around is not to keep too many friends and know who to choose as your friends.

Today, I got my dinner at about 11:30. Imagine having your Sunday dinner from 12 p.m. On a daily basis, we would have breakfast at about 10, dinner at 11:30, and supper at 2:30; that would be for the day. On the nights you would have to purchase a snack before lockdown. There is a song that has been in my head from jail:

"Have you any river that seems uncrossable

God specializes in things impossible

He'll do for you what no other can do."

August 18, 2008- My Grandfather Passed Away

Today, I woke up feeling a bit miserable. I did what I had to, then I went to the tailor shop. This kind of living is getting to me; almost all the inmates on the section I'm located on are juveniles (most of the older ones have been transferred or placed on another section). Plus, having to live with constant searches is stressful. For it seems that for the past couple of months that I have been here, a man has been taken to prison every day. And this is only one of the prisons! I thank God for my family in these trying times...almost every day I wake up, there is a fight inside the prison or something else going wrong.

Today was my visiting day. I wasn't expecting any visitors, but an orderly approached my cell and said I should pack up my plates as I had a visitor. I got dressed and went to see who it was. It was my uncle. The visiting boxes were tiny, and I could hardly hear a word because other inmates spoke loudly. My uncle told me that my grandfather had passed (my mother's father). Although, he and I weren't very close, I would still miss him, and I knew that my mom would need our support. I felt terrible for two reasons. Firstly, I lost another family member, and it was heart-wrenching not to show support. Secondly, I won't even be able to make it to the funeral because of someone else's lie. A lie that placed me in this situation that deprived me of basic needs…. to be able to be physically present with loved ones, the thought alone is sometimes depressing.

July 9, 2009

Today started like any other day. It has been a year and two months since I've been here. So much has changed and happened during the period which felt like years. I've lost a lot of weight. I've matured. I'm giving God thanks for so much. We have been searched by warders, police, soldiers, etc. There was also a rumor that a prisoner had a gun in the prison, which resulted in another big search. That day, I was in my cell from 3:00 PM the previous day until about 1:00 PM the following afternoon. Life has been rough, but I'm coping. There have been times that I reached the point of giving up. I don't want to see anyone, but my parents and friends.

There are times when I feel so bad inside but I'm trying to keep the faith, even though there are so many reasons to give up. Life comes at you fast, so you just have to know how to handle it. When I came to prison, I used to question my circumstances, but I realized it made no sense. The Lord, sometimes, puts us in situations and He wants us to be His answer for that specific situation. However, the most amazing part is I'm alive to give Him thanks. I'm happy I woke up with a head that could hurt. Many inmates went to bed and never had the chance to glimpse light again. 'Better to be a patient man than a warrior.'

April 9, 2009

My week started fairly well, but yesterday, I heard some news, not good information or necessary either. I found out that I appealed my conviction so I am not serving a sentence. This means that if I lose out on my appeal that is when my sentence would start. That's unbelievable. So, I haven't started serving my sentence all this time, which is so unfair.

Since being in prison, I notified the authorities of my election to work even though I'm an appellant. When someone has been convicted appeals his/her sentence, that individual is not considered as serving a sentence but rather a remand. So, each day that goes by doesn't count. So, I'm not, therefore, eligible to work. So, therefore, I had to write a letter to the superintendent in charge asking for permission stating that if I'm injured, or anything of that sort, in the process of working, they would not be liable for any damages. I attended classes inside the prison where I studied Principles of Business, Mathematics, and Computer Graphics. I'm also learning tailoring and assisting in making uniforms for the warders. In my perception, I do not see prison as a place of rehabilitation, as prisoners spend their time contemplating how they are going to get even with whosoever sent them there. But not all prisoners are like that, some are genuinely sorry, while some show no remorse.

I've learned that, in life, we never get more than what we can bear. The first week I came here, someone told me prison is like a bomb, you never know when it will explode. Plus, you do not know what to expect each day.

I just have to give thanks for each day that I make it through alive. I would not want my worst enemy to come to a place like this. I wonder how the young lady feels within herself knowing she sent an innocent man to prison. I wonder if she has a heart. I have stopped writing and reading lately because of my level of depression. Through all of this, I still have to give God thanks. I do not know what's in store for me for the future. So, I'm living a day at a time. Without prayers, I don't know where I would be right now. I try my best to read my Bible regularly. Whatever your situation is; never give up. If God brings you to it, He will get you through it.

July 8, 2009

Today is said to be a perfect day because, in approximately 12 hours, 34 minutes, 56 seconds, the world will go through a particular time that occurs roughly every 50 years.

LETTER FROM MY MOTHER:

September 29, 2009

*Dear Mrs. *Young*

I write in reference to the case of Kevaughn Irving which I have referred to you for handling his appeal.

I would like to bring to your attention concerns I have regarding the representation, or lack thereof, by his then-Attorney, Mr. Lucas Jordan, whose services I had retained for handling the matter in the lower court.*

During the trial, I had on several occasions inquired of Mr. Jordan whether or not I could make a contribution or present any evidence in preparing for the hearing. On all these occasions, I was told by Mr. Jordan to "leave my case alone", or that he had all grounds covered. This form of defensive behaviour, on the part of Mr. Jordan, started quite early in the case. Kevaughn was locked up in Spanish Town for four days without being charged. I was advised that there were grounds that Mr. Jordan could have used for his release of 'habeas corpus', and I advised him of such and was met with the same resistance. During this period, I had expressed my concerns to my sister, Sharon, who was instrumental in my retention of Mr. Jordan. On March 27, 2008, I met with Mr. Jordan to pay a portion of his fee and discuss the way forward on the matter, which was set for April 1, 2008. Mr. Jordan advised both Kevaughn and me that he had received the DNA results and according to him, there was nothing linking Kevaughn to the rape. I, at that point, tried to discuss with him matters of discrepancies, which I had noted in the claim made by the complainant. He again bluntly told me that I don't need to advise him of discrepancies as he had his case covered. What was more surprising was that he advised me that he does not discuss his case with his client's parents. I then informed him to talk to Kevaughn about the case. Nothing was discussed.

The trial started on April 2, 2008. Since I could not be in the courtroom, I was advised by Kevaughn that the plaintiff claimed that he was picked up in Bog Walk when he was actually picked up by the criminals in Angels Spanish Town. I had the receipts and the medication I had sent Kevaughn to purchase in my possession. The following day, I gave Kevaughn these receipts, plus the box that contained the medication he was sent to purchase. It contained the date and the location of the pharmacy where the purchase was made. I also gave him my updated bankbook which showed the withdrawals that were made on the said date. Kevaughn was put on the stand and Mr. Jordan presented these documents which were accepted into evidence at that late stage.

Another major concern I have is the fact that I saw Mr. Jordan conversing alone with the complainant. When he met with us a short while after, he told us that she advised him that she knew Kevaughn and she had, in fact, called him to tell him to give himself up.

Kevaughn was taken back into custody on April 9, 2008. I became aware of the importance of character witnesses when I was questioned by several people if character witnesses were being called to court. Several people stood ready to do so including police officers, lecturers, students, and church members. At this point, I contacted the schools he attended and received documents confirming his attendance. These are the documents I have since submitted to you.

I would also like to refer to the attached letter from Mr. Jordan to the Jamaicans for Justice. The tone of the letter speaks volumes about the attitude displayed during the trial.

The question may be asked why I continued with his service despite my concerns. I had, in fact, consulted another lawyer with the intention of making changes but could not because of cost considerations and we had already committed to using Mr. Jordan. Mr. Jordan also came with high commendation, and, therefore, despite my concerns, I maintained him as my lawyer.

My son now sits behind the walls of the General Penitentiary, surprised discouraged that the very justice system that should be protecting him has actually failed him. A victim he was and has now become the accused. As a mother of two teenagers, I now have the task of assuring my other children that the justice system does work.

The learned Judge erred in her judgment. My son's lawyer, Mr. Jordan, did not perform his job as a defense attorney, which resulted in a miscarriage of justice. He had several avenues that could have been explored and investigated that he did not use, and his attitude was not accommodating. I have referred this matter to you because I still have confidence in the system, your ability, and your integrity. I ask that you explore all avenues to ensure that justice is served.

Respectfully yours,

Client and Distressed Mother

September 2, 2009

It's my second birthday in this deplorable place; now, it's getting to me, the height of corruption. Some people in prison only talk to you because you are kind enough to give them something. It is just a matter of time until my time is up; I can't wait to leave. I miss my family badly, and sometimes, I want to give up and just disappear. However, I have to be strong for my family and myself. When I got out of my cell, I had breakfast, had a shower, and ate my dinner. I stayed in the cell for most of the day. Today seemed like every other day; there was nothing to celebrate.

September 28, 2009

Today is the day my appeal goes to court; it started pretty crazy. When the section was unlocked, a series of events took place in the following order:

There was no water → Fight downstairs → Fight on my section → Fight at Boys Town leaving one dead.

It has been quite a morning so far, so bad that the whole prison has been placed under lockdown. I made sure I stayed in my cell, awaiting my fate in the Court of Appeal.

January 12, 2010 – A DAY TO REMEMBER

People often say that "Jamaicans are bad lucky and poor", but we are one of the most blessed islands in the world At about 4:53 PM, I was in my cell lying down when suddenly I felt the place begin shaking. I could actually see and feel the building shaking; I could actually see and feel the building swaying side-to-side. The shake lasted for approximately 20 seconds. I was very frightened because it was the first time, I had experienced a tremor of that magnitude. Two nights prior to the quake, we were told the country had a cold front. There is a saying which goes "no matter how bad things are going for you, someone has it worse."

While our blessed little island experienced a minor tremor, the same earthquake, a magnitude 7 in size, was destroyed the island of Haiti. Those 20 seconds seemed like an eternity. A total of over 100,000 people were feared dead, and the death toll was still rising. Being incarcerated and there is an earthquake is a terrifying feeling because you cannot move around, and you are confined to one particular place. Yet, it teaches you the discipline to cope under the circumstances.

A few weeks earlier, an American Airline passenger plane overshot ran the runway at the Normally Manley International Airport. The aircraft broke into three pieces. All passengers and crew survived the crash...another miracle. The crash was due to an error by the pilot; he was advised by the control tower not to land on that particular runway due to poor lighting. He also erred because he landed the aircraft some 4,000 plus feet on the airstrip that was 8,000 plus feet. When I read the daily paper, I wondered what if a tsunami or one of these natural disasters should hit our beloved island. How would we as prisoners get through being locked up like dogs? Before arriving at G.P, I was told about an attempted escape that left a few prisoners and warders dead. Consequently, the prison went on lockdown and soldiers were called in.

January 19, 2010 THINGS & TIMES CHANGING

Today started just like any other day, but one can never have a normal day in prison. One thing that changed my day was that I read a newspaper article about a pregnant 10-year-old who gave birth, and the baby died three weeks later. The shocking part is the fact that she conceived for a man in his 30s. When I read the article, I asked myself how a man in his right mind could be attracted to a 10-year-old child.

When I first glanced at the article a particular scripture came to mind which spoke about children giving birth to children. I smiled and said to myself that the Bible is fulfilling. I despise men who take advantage of women and children.

January 25, 2010

There is a saying, which goes 'there is no place like home', and I found that to be true. Over the past couple of days, I have gotten so frustrated. Life seems so meaningless. Today, I went to the 'tuck shop' and a warder confiscated my PSP (handheld game). I was so shocked as I was told they caught other prisoners trying to access the Internet with the games. Because of that, they confiscated it. I was taken to the overseer's office and the acting superintendent told the warder to charge me. Prison life is so unfair.

I am not a troublemaker and I have never crossed the line with fellow inmates or warders, yet trouble has crossed my path so many times. I'm not a time-waster, so I try to keep myself occupied by reading or writing in my journal. I can't even seem to be bothered with this journal, but I have to tell my life story to the whole world. There are so many reasons to give up. Prison isn't a bed of roses; however, I try my best to make myself comfortable with my situation.

March 3, 2010

I woke up today feeling so frustrated about my situation. I'm tired of being in this godforsaken place. I got up and started tidying the cell. A warder came to my cell and asked me my name and where I worked in the prison. I answered him and he proceeded to say, "I should push out the phone." I told him I didn't have a phone. He then told me he was going to search my cell. So, my cellmates and I came out and he went in. The man ransacked every single thing in the cell.

The strangest thing was that my cell was the only one that was searched and there were no other warders present to supervise this so-called 'search'. The warder further stated that another warder had made a report to the superintendent and that the superintendent sent him for the phone. I was the only one on the section whose cell was searched.

I keep thinking, 'In God, I trust so it's 'mind over matter.'

May 4, 2010

My heart is heavy. My head is confused. I feel as if I no longer know what to do. I'm feeling stressed and all alone. My head is so packed up with so many things. All I can do is give thanks for life and pray for a bright future ahead of me...with God all things are possible.

September 17, 2010 (COURT DAY)

It's been two years and six months since I've been here. Today is my day so I prepared all my clothes and stuff for court the day before. I got up early and got myself ready. We, however, had to wait for the police to come and pick us up. My name was called, and I was taken downstairs and the warders handed me over to the police. There were six of us going to court that morning. We were cuffed and placed in the vehicle to be escorted to the courthouse. The journey took approximately 10 minutes. Upon arrival, we were thoroughly searched and taken to the holding area; a feeling of anxiousness came over me. I listened as the other inmates related their ordeals. Shortly afterward my name was called to go to the courtroom. I was handcuffed with another prisoner and taken to the courtroom.

The case was called up, and my new lawyer got up. The lawyer got up. She spoke with authority as she asked the judge for bail. The judge asked the prosecution if she had any objection to which she said no. So, the judge offered me bail, but at that particular time, the court's office was now closed. I felt a load being lifted. Not the justice I wanted, but I knew that I would be going home. I was taken back to the prison and taken to my cell. I told my cellmates about the events that had taken place. They seemed happy for me. I was so glad that night, I could hardly sleep. I packed all my bags and began counting down the hours, which seemed like an eternity. I, however, didn't let that break me because I knew I was going home tomorrow. I was released about 4:00 PM that afternoon, and I felt as if I could scream freedom. I was not 100% free, but I knew I would not have to spend another night in a prison cell, and I would finally go home to my family and friends.

My uncle and mom came to pick me up. I was so relieved to be going home. Throughout my ordeal, I never once shed a tear openly, instead, I kept it in. It hurt like hell though to know I was incarcerated for being in the wrong place at the wrong time. But I learned a valuable lesson – one has to give thanks for their freedom. Sometimes, the smallest things we take for granted can become the biggest mistake of our lives. One should also appreciate family and friends, especially a mother. We may have a million and one friends, but we get one mother.

I knew that after I was incarcerated, my life would by no means be the same. Every day I wake up, I give thanks for life and for just being free.

CHAPTER THIRTEEN

Finally Home...

It has been a year and a few months since I was released on bail. Still trying to pick up the pieces of my life, I was often left feeling like I was barely making progress. And, there was still an obstacle in my way – I was a convicted felon with a criminal record, accused and found guilty of a crime I did not commit.

Since being released, I have been to court on numerous occasions and reported to the police station twice per week. I was more confident with this new lawyer. In addition, the Jamaicans for Justice organisation also stepped in as my defense. I could not seem to obtain a job because I was convicted. I did several interviews in which I was successful, but I had a police record.

It has been tough but as the saying goes "prayer moves mountains". I was broken emotionally, but thank God He sent his son Jesus to die for me.

Unfortunately, I came home with the wrong impression. I came home expecting to have my family's help financially, but that did not work out as I had hoped. The whole situation broke them; it depleted whatever savings they had accumulated over the years. They were now in debt due to visits and paying the lawyer's fees.

On my first visit to the court, the prosecutor who did the first trial asked to be removed because she believed it was an unfair trial. I thought that was a huge sign that things would eventually work in my favour.

There were times when I felt as if I didn't want to go on, but I had to push for two reasons: God gives us tests so we can have testimonies, and, sometimes, we have trials and temptations. But when we are ready to give up, that's when the Lord gives us our breakthrough. Just having faith can determine the outcome. God can take our mess and give us a message, but first, we have to submit ourselves totally to Him.

It has been almost two years since I had been out, and it has really been a rough road, but I had to give thanks. I asked the Lord to place me in a similar situation. Why? Out of anger, I suppose. I wanted to see how I would react to being in the same position again. Standing at 6 feet 2, weighing over 200 pounds, how would I now exert my fear and anger if three men abducted me? The whole trauma of what I'd gone through had taken such a toll on my life. I became a more reserved person.

I had also been searching so hard for love instead of just letting go and letting God lead. I had been through so many relationships. I really couldn't seem to settle down. I couldn't seem to find someone to understand me. I loved my life but hated the way I was living. At times, I even wished I didn't survive the whole ordeal.

Since being released, I tried rededicating my life to the Lord, but I honestly felt there was something still missing in my life. My family was devastated by the whole situation. The entire case had taken a toll on them; it cost them their years of life savings plus a lot more. I tried hard to hold back the tears at times because I had come too far to let go.

CHAPTER FOURTEEN

New Life

A little over two years had passed since my release, and I decided it was now time to rededicate my life to the Lord. I was re-baptized and gave my all to the Lord. The Christian pathway was narrow and winding, filled with many obstacles and tribulations. But, with Jehovah, God as the pilot, I was safe. I still asked the question, 'Why me, oh Lord?' Yet, the amazing part was that I kept my sanity, and I forgave the young lady for lying even though she still insisted that I was involved. Honestly, I prayed she would stop before the Lord intervened. True forgiveness comes from within. I had to truly forgive her to let go of the pain holding me captive, like a prisoner in my own body.

Life had been a rough road. The road to Christianity was challenging, but the Lord did not give me more than I could bear. The job-hunting seemed futile; it was difficult to obtain a job because I now had a criminal record. Jamaicans believed that we were all the same when someone went to prison. Guilty or innocent, we were all considered to be the same.

I was the convicted rapist, murderer, robber, madman, innocent man locked behind bars. Society will stereotype me, categorize me, and keep me in a box. I sometimes wondered if the system would still treat me like a criminal when I was acquitted?

CHAPTER FIFTEEN

Love

What is love? Love can be defined simply as a strong feeling of affection, great interest, or pleasure in something. How does one love or find love after being traumatised, framed, and broken-hearted? After prison, I couldn't live my life how I wanted. Nevertheless, the Lord gave me the strength to move, breathe, inhale, and the body to do anything and everything. I knew it would prevail in this case, and I would find the right woman for me. I continued to magnify Him, but sometimes, there were periods of loneliness. I met a lot of young ladies after I was released, and it seemed that I had been searching for love in all the wrong places.

Somewhere along the way, I met a fascinating young lady. It was love at first sight. She stands elegantly at five feet and three inches with beautiful chocolate skin. What I also loved about her were her personality and spirit. There was one problem with her: she doubted herself. She was beautiful, and she told herself she wasn't. I met her mother and siblings. They accepted me with open arms. I visited them regularly, feeling as if this was my second home. I loved her, and there was nothing we kept from each other. She had a beautiful baby boy, and I treated him as if he was my own. She was also timid, but there was something about her I couldn't understand, but I just left it as it was. We were together for a few months, and we never thought there would be heartbreak between us. She also met my mom. It was almost a year since we had been together when I found out the real purpose of myself in her life, which was to serve as a means of motivation for her. So, we decided we would call it quits, and we both moved on with our lives. A part of me left with her. Imagine life like this: each time you meet someone, you think they are your everything, and then, somewhere down the line, that person leaves. A part of you gets broken.

Sometimes you realise that you are broken or damaged but still blame someone else for the previous person's mistake. Consequently, you will never love anyone else like you loved the first person. Love is fabulous, but it hurts very badly when you lose it. Another big issue that destroys relationships is closure. If one cannot let go of previous relationships, then another cannot prosper until we let go of the past. There is one thing Monique, and I managed to salvage from the relationship, and that was our friendship.

CHAPTER SIXTEEN

A Saturday To Remember

Almost two years after my release on bail, I finally landed a job. The management of a supermarket and auto parts store wanted me to have a second chance, so they hired me. I was employed there as a store assistant.

One Saturday, I should have been in church; instead, I was at work breaking yet another Sabbath, which I knew I shouldn't be doing. Anyway, I made it through the day. It was now time for me to go home. I waited for about an hour before I got a bus. I arrived at one of the bus stops and stepped off the bus. I boarded another bus and sat next to the door. After a couple of minutes, the vehicle was full, and the bus drove off with the conductor standing at the door. Upon reaching a section of the road, two men boarded the bus and pushed past the conductor; these men were dressed as gangsters.

My heart raced. My body began shaking. How is this happening to me again, I began to think? I let my eyes search the floor, and I quietly prayed for swift intervention. Not only did I pray for it, I believed in God for it. I lifted my head and watched the men.

The men's eyes searched the bus looking at every passenger. I let their eyes meet mine. I watched as one of them greeted one of the passengers seated at the back of the bus. The passenger asked him what he was doing on the bus, but the men stopped the bus after a few minutes and came off. Sometime after that, we realised that the man the men greeted was an off-duty policeman.

So, it seemed the men wanted to rob the bus but were deterred by the police officer on board. It was yet another blessing from God. I was almost in a similar situation as before, and I was positive I would have dealt with the situation differently. Thanks be to God. Be careful what you ask for, as you might get it.

CHAPTER SEVENTEEN

Sweet Alecia

Born on the 9th of June 1992, Alecia grew up with her Mom. Her father didn't play a significant role in her life. She stands six feet tall, slim, and sexy. She has a heart of a lamb and one filled with love and humbleness. When I first met her, I thought she was just pretending, so I told myself I would just play along. I had lost most of my love towards females due to the previous incident, but I sensed something different about Alecia. Soon after, I was happy to have met her. She was the only one who accepted me for who I was and not my physique or status.

On our first date, we went to the zoo, and it was then I realised that she was not going to be just my friend. Alecia's Mom was a very hard-working woman, and she worked hard to make ends meet for her children. She tried to give them the life she never had. Being the last of her siblings, Alecia was spoiled. Her eldest sister was also a caregiver, having made provisions for Alecia to attend college. So she could have a good education and hence get a well-paying job.

When I met Alecia, she was a third-year student in college and stressed. Yet, she was able to teach me true love and how to appreciate the little I have. Her family readily accepted me, having heard of my past. Although we were not stable financially, that didn't stop our love from growing steadily within a matter of months. Regular arguments strengthened our love. I wanted to marry her and spend the rest of my life with her. I was, however, embarrassed as I was not able to financially support her as I should. I am a firm believer that a man should be a provider and protector for his family.

Three critical components are the foundation of a successful relationship. I refer to them as the 3Cs:

Compromise: To compromise is to come to a mutual agreement where each party relinquishes a part of their demands or beliefs.

Communication: Good communication provides lasting relationships driven by trust, honesty, and respect.

Commitment: An intentional decision to be dedicated to someone despite challenges.

With these three, any relationship will work, but it will prosper with God in the midst. Alecia accepted me, although I had nothing to offer at the time but my love. She loved on me even though she knew I had a court case, and I appreciated her for that. This book would not have been possible without her unwavering support.

Since we met, she has attended almost every court appointment with me. What more could a man ask for? BESIDE EVERY SUCCESSFUL MAN, THERE IS A STRONG WOMAN. To all men, if you find a woman willing to stick with you through the bad times, love her through the good times because chances are she is ready to spend the rest of her life with you.

CHAPTER EIGHTEEN

Aftermath

Since the incident, my whole life has been traumatised. Nevertheless, my family has supported me 100 percent. My mother had sleepless nights, and my father had not gotten over the ordeal yet. The whole case had left us in debt. Imagine a life of paying for a crime that you were a victim of. I started doubting women at one point that they are all liars, but prayer brought me through that hurt.

To each court appearance, I was accompanied by my parents, aunt, or girlfriend. In addition, other family members and close friends would call just to find out what was happening or to show their support. On numerous occasions, the matter had to be postponed due to one of the defendants being absent.

At a particular court appearance, I heard that the girl was in fear, so she did not come to court. I was so shocked, and I wondered to myself what or whom she was afraid of? My only conclusion was her conscience. Each time I attended court, and the matter was put off; bus fare was wasted. Plus, it's time for closure to this case, and it's only a matter of time before the truth sets me completely FREE!!!

CHAPTER NINETEEN

Insanity Or What?

My dear readers, while I was writing this book, I realised how truly broken I was. ***Prescription to Prison*** made me realise the reality of my life. I will never live a normal life, as this whole ordeal has changed my perception. On numerous occasions, I wished I never existed. I felt as if a part of my life was missing. Most nights, I am unable to fall asleep before midnight. I managed to keep my feelings bottled up inside. So many times, I just felt like breaking down and crying, but the man inside wouldn't allow me.

It tore me apart, knowing I did not do such a crime and having to pay for it was unbearable. Each time I had to go to the police station and report, I felt as if I was a criminal. Some family members were clueless about what I was facing as I managed to hide my feelings with a smile. I explained it to them when I felt up to it; although I had already cost them so much, I didn't want to burden them, with my mental roller coaster of emotions.

There were also times when I just wanted to lock myself in a room and just scream. I was broken, but I still had to try and put my best forward. Depression affects everyone at some point in their journey. Due to the ordeal, I felt mightily depressed most times. Imagine living a life unsure of a future. Living a life in the fate of Jamaica's Justice System. Every day, I prayed that the girl would just come forward and tell the truth. I prayed for that and asked the Lord to forgive her for her lies.

My time behind bars showed me the reality of Jamaica's Judiciary System. Some officers carried out little or no investigation in cases, thus sending many young men behind bars.

Being charged with five offences is too much for one person to bear, especially knowing that I may have to return to prison and start my time all over again. *"What then," I ask myself...What then"*

CHAPTER TWENTY

A Change Will Soon Come

April 4, 2014, marked seven years since the incident that changed my life forever. On my last court appearance on the 1st of April, the case was again postponed due to the absence of the woman. She was also absent on the previous occasion. The whole thing has been so frustrating; I am still unable to obtain a decent job because I have a criminal record. I am also unable to travel outside of Jamaica. It's as if every step I take forward, I take two steps backward.

In the meantime, I wanted to return to the classroom. To learn a new skill that would provide for better job opportunities my grandmother (my mother's mother) provided the means for me to do so, to go back to school to learn another skill of my choice. After careful thinking, I decided to try something new, so I enrolled in an electrical installation programme. A very technical course but not beyond learning, plus there were advantages to gaining certification in this career field. I would be learning a new skill; it would also make me more marketable in an already competitive workforce. However, there were also challenges involved. I was afraid of electricity, and I wasn't very good at Mathematics or Technical Drawing. I succeeded at it and made my family proud. I am open-minded to learn something new. I also had to remain focused during the programme, which included a lot of assignments and research. At the end of my tenure at the institution, I was awarded a level three certification, which is also internationally recognized.

2015

The year 2015 was a very hectic year for me. I have been depressed, the reason being that I have not been able to find a job. My once bright smile has been transformed into a sad, somewhat depressing frown. Deep in my heart, I am still trying to hold on. Where there was love, there is now a buildup of anger, insecurity, and a feeling of uncertainty. Through the midst of all my trials, I still tried to put on a smile on others' faces. It is so hard trying to keep it all together. I barely sleep at night due to thoughts of my life being wasted as the court case continues to drag on without no victory. But through it all, I believe in a God who is everywhere at once, one who knows everything. He is the author and finisher of my faith. I hope that all my trials and tribulations aren't meant for nothing, but rather, I see them as obstacles put in front of me to make me a stronger man. So, instead of complaining about my ordeal, I give thanks for making it through alive. I am angry, yes, but nothing beats anger. I may seem like I have it under control, but the truth is I'm just living my life one day at a time. Whatever the outcome is… I'm ready.

I Want Justice!!

New year, the same blues; 2017 was a bittersweet year. I can't help but say thank God. The challenges were many, and they came rapidly close. In November 2017, the case was again called up and put off.

Towards the end of the year, tragedy struck. Firstly, a close friend hung himself leaving his friends and family members devastated. A week later, gunmen murdered my stepbrother in broad daylight, leaving his little girl fatherless. The crime rate in Jamaica is spiraling out of control. The country needs divine intervention. Through all the everyday trials, I am still giving thanks to God for life, good friends, and family. With those things, I know I am unstoppable.

However, I have concluded that there is no justice in our court system in Jamaica. On numerous occasions, I have been to the courthouse only to hear that the matter is being put off for reasons such as the investigating officer being absent, the witness's non-appearance, or files not being ready. There are days when I honestly feel depressed and frustrated because the system is wasting my life away!

The incident took place in 2007. I went to prison exactly one year later. I did two years and five months at GP. Ten years since the incident and worse, seven years after being out on bail, still no retrial. No justice on my behalf. There is no care for a young man's life from humble beginnings living on this island.

The woman who claimed I raped her, I often wondered what was her motive behind it all. I also realised that the investigating officer was now a witness in the matter. There are days when I blame myself for all that I was going through. If I had never reported the matter, I could not have gone to prison for a crime I did not commit. Forensic evidence taken from the victim was never sent to the lab until some 10 to 14 days after they were taken from the victim. Nothing was done to preserve them.

Therefore, I'm left to question the integrity of our police force regarding the level of investigation carried out when a crime is committed or is it that both statements are taken, then they decide on which side to take. I am not saying this applies to the entire force, but it seems to have become a trend in our police force.

Being before the courts has basically put my life on a downward spiral, firstly, I had to surrender my travel documents, now my expired passport is somewhere at the Spanish Town Courts Office and cannot be renewed until the matter ends. Secondly, it has proven to be difficult or impossible to obtain a clean police record, which is needed when seeking employment from several reputable companies in Jamaica.

With that said, I gained employment with a company at which I was now serving for the past three years. Thankfully they decided to give me a chance and risk employing me; since then, I have proven to be an asset instead of a liability. I was working at the wharf, which significantly improved my living standard. I was also able to learn the intricacies of the shipping and export industry.

CHAPTER TWENTY-ONE

Beginning Of Retrial

Monday, April 29, 2019

Day 1-3

Finally, the retrial has started. This morning, I got up, and finally, the retrial began. I arrived at the courthouse around 9:45 a.m. The judge came shortly after; my lawyer was late, so the case was stood down. After a few minutes, my lawyer arrived, and the retrial started.

The girl (complainant) was the first on the stand and was sworn in. In her recount of the incident, she said she stopped the car at Bog walk roundabout and went in on the back seat. She said, it was her and the driver alone in the car. The car later made a stop at a stoplight where four men then entered on the back seat with her, two on the left and two on the right, leaving the front seat empty. She said she knew me as Mr. Biggs, and she also claimed the driver was the first to pull a gun on her. The girl also told the court that the car stopped under a traffic light, and that was when she saw the other men's gun. I told the men my Grandma had land in the area and directed the men there. *"A inform you a carry wi fi inform pan man,"* she claimed. She further stated the men then took the gun from me and hit me with the gun in my neck. She went on to say they then took us back in the car, where they drove some more into the bushes. She also claimed that she grabbed onto my testicles and squeezed hard, and I cried out to the men if they would let the woman kill me. She said the driver came and pointed the gun in her forehead, then she let go. When she saw me at the police station, she pulled a chair to hit me, and a police officer pulled a gun on her and told her to put it down. However, in the retrial, she said the officer calmly told her to put down the chair.

During cross-examination, she proceeded to tell her lies making them even more dramatic at each of her recounts of the incident. The cross-examination continued for another day and the court put on recess until May 14, 2019.

Tuesday, May 14, 2019

Continuation of Retrial

I got up early this morning but got caught in traffic. I was worried that I may reach court late, however, I arrived 10 minutes before ten. I went in and saw a note on the door which said the court was resuming at 2:00 p.m. so I waited until about 1:45 p.m., then I went inside the courtroom. The complainant was sworn in, and the cross-examination began. The lawyer asked her why she gave two different stories under oath. While trying to explain, she complained of feeling ill and asked for a tissue, and the court clerk assisted her. A few minutes later, the complainant complained that her head was feeling a bit giddy in the cross-questioning. So, the judge asked if she was feeling ok enough to continue the trial; her response was *"I'll try ma'am"*, however, the judge sent her outside to get some fresh air. Upon entering the courthouse, the complainant opened the door and almost fainted and had to be escorted out. The police officer assisted her to the bench to lay down. Minutes later, she passed out and had to be rushed to the hospital by the police, unresponsive.

In deliberation, the case was further put off until a later date and my bail until then was extended. Looking back, if there were anything I could have done to help her, I would but if I did, possibilities are I would have been killed. It's unfair, however, that we were both victims and she insisted that I was a part of the whole thing. We may think life is unfair but God has a way of working things in our favour.

There is a saying in Jamaica *"wah nuh dead nuh dash it weh"*, this means from there is life anything is possible.

There are two things that make you rich in this life; you can have a lot of money or a lot of friends but you can never have both.

December 2019

It's the end of another year, my case is still in the court, it has really been a challenging year financially and emotionally. . It's been tough having to go to court but sitting in the courtroom and listening to the woman constantly lying. It's terrible not being able to confront her about it is another issue, but God knows best.

On my last court appearance, the woman was still being cross-examined, in the final entry to the court, the prosecutor asked the woman why is it her statement was constantly changing. Initially, she told the court I was the first one to rape her, then in the retrial, she changed her statement and said I was the last one to rape her. She explained that she didn't alter really change up her statement, so the matter had to be set for another date. It is a heart-wrenching feeling to have to sit in the courtroom and listen to someone telling lies, and you have to sit and listen through it all.

I have trusted the Lord through it all, and I'm by no means ready to give up on Him. Life is filled with challenges, and how one faces them determines his/her outcome, but as I said; God will not put us in any situation that He does not intend to give us a blessing or a lesson. This case has been a vital part of all decisions regarding my freedom. I have not allowed my current situation to determine my outcome.

The crime rate in Jamaica is spiraling uncontrollably; even under the current State of Emergency (SOE), persons are still being murdered. A lot of families have been torn apart due to gang and political violence. Every day is a funeral, and it's mostly young people. I pray for my family and friends daily. Going out and coming home safe is something to be thankful for.

2019 Summary

The year 2019 has been more than a rough year. It has been filled with a lot of ups and downs. I've been really trying to cope mentally, financially, and emotionally with my current situation. I hardly ever go out for enjoyment. The crime rate has risen higher than in 2018. The Zone of Special

Operations (ZOSO) has been extended in several parishes, and they are unable to keep the crime rate down. It is alarming as to the brazen killing taking place in little Jamaica, but that's the reality of it. I myself have gotten frustrated with the court and justice system. Having to go to court on each occasion has been very frustrating. I can't wait to hear it's over.

My biggest fear, however, is that this case is making me into a bitter person. In reality, this case has made me so angry deep inside being unable to move towards my dream. I feel confined, not being able to do what I dreamed of, due to the fact that I cannot travel or obtain a clean police record. I fear that one day I won't be able to control my feelings because the least of things gets me upset, the smallest things, and I'm afraid people I value may walk out of my life because of that fact.

I've considered getting counseling; having to deal with the pressures of work, home, and court sometimes feels a bit overwhelming. There are so many people I can talk to but yet, I still keep it bottled up inside, it's a very scary feeling, I really do not want to end up sad, alone, and angry with the world or the people in it.

The Lord has been good to me in the sense that He has spared my life thus far to see another year – 2020. He has also given me the strength to keep moving forward and to slowly let go of my past. Without the help of certain family and friends, I could not have made it this far. Their constant encouragement has pushed me forward, although being depressed at times. I appreciated all the prayers, text messages, and everything they have done to put a smile on my face.

February 2020

Who The Lord Sets Free…

I've been to court, and on the previous occasion, a no-case submission was filed by my attorney. She made submissions that the prosecutor had no case against me; there were too many inconsistencies to make the case a fair retrial. My lawyer also stated that the prosecutor chose to withhold vital documents that would have made the case even much easier, even though it may or may not weaken the crown's case. However, in her response to my lawyer's no-case submission, the crown told the court that it could have been a possibility that I knew the girl, and I knew that she knew me, so that was possibly one of the reasons why I went to make a report at the station. However, the judge said it could also have been a possibility that I genuinely didn't know the complainant and went on to let the crown know that she wasn't a 'possibilities' judge.

After responding to my lawyer's submission, the presiding judge said she needed some time to go over all the evidence. Then said, she would make her ruling as to whether or not she will accept the submission.

February 7, 2020

Free At Last - Judge's Final Decision!!!

I got up this morning anxiously waiting on 12:00 p.m. as that is the time the judge should hand down her ruling on whether or not she accepted the submissions made by my lawyer.

The court was called to order, and I sat and listened as the judge passed down her judgment. I listened to every word said; the room was so tense.

JUDGE'S RULING

The absence of certain evidence was one of the bases for the submissions by the Defense that the Court should exercise its inherent jurisdiction and not call on the accused to answer to the charges because of the unfairness of this trial.

Another basis for the submissions of no case to answer is that the prosecution's case is riddled with inconsistencies. In considering that basis, I bear in mind that some 12 years have passed since the crime has been committed, and these same memories must have faded. Here, I remind myself that the prosecution cannot be forced or directed to present or agree on evidence. The responsibility rests on the prosecution to determine the manner in which to present the case, the witnesses to be called, and the order in which they are to be called. At the same time, and I think first, it is entitled to a fair trial, which includes access to available evidence which is under the control of the prosecution. The recognition of this is seen in several authorities, which requires the prosecution to make a disclosure to the defense. Here, the defense submits that the prosecution has failed to provide important pertinent evidence that the accused has thus been deprived of a fair trial and that he should not, therefore, be called to answer to the charges. Included in this omitted evidence, according to the defense, are statements from the security guards and from first respondents, which could have at least provided evidence of the complainant's initial condition and first utterances after the alleged incident.

The defense acknowledges that the complainant was the victim of a crime but maintains that it was not committed by the accused, who himself was a victim of abduction, according to them. Therefore, in my view, the case should not be stopped for those particular omissions as to the initial conditions and utterances.

The defense submits further that scientific and documentary evidence is available, which could show that the accused was not a participant in the crime. It seems it could weaken the prosecution's case or strengthen the defense's case. The defense argument includes a station diary entry and the forensic and scientific tests of the complainant's and the accused bodily fluids. This could be vital in view of the evidence that the accused ejaculated inside of the complainant and that swabs of bodily fluid were taken from both for scientific analysis and I have acknowledged that memories must have failed and recognized that such failure would occur not only in the memory of the crown's witness but also those of the accused. Scientific and documentary evidence does not alter with the passage of time, and it can assist both the crown and defense when available.

In my judgment, by not providing important, pertinent, available evidence, including scientific and documentary evidence. The case presented by the crown is incomplete. The crown may have reasons for these omissions, but to my mind, these omissions result in an unfair trial.

The prosecution must present relevant and pertinent evidence or make it available whether or not it supports the prosecution's case. Where the prosecution chooses not to so present, the judge, in my view, has a duty to protect the right of the accused to have a fair trial. That must be, to me, letting him be privity to and have access to all relevant evidence. Here, I seriously view the omissions in this case, and having considered the entirety of the case presented, I will not call on the accused to answer. I so rule in order to prevent an unfair trial Mr. Irving, the verdict I am entering is Not Guilty, meaning there is no case to answer. You are free to go on these charges.

When I heard that, an instant load was lifted off my shoulders. I was happy. In telling the judge, thank you, water filled my eyes. It was finally over, just two months shy of almost 13 years since the incident. I wanted to scream and run out of the courtroom, but I held my composure, a sigh of relief. Both my lawyers were overwhelmed as the case was finally over after ten years.

On the outside of the courthouse, home, and abroad family members were overwhelmed at hearing of my victory.

It could have only been God at work.

So, I complete the final chapter in this book, first and foremost, I just want to thank God Almighty again for making me victorious after almost 13 years. My attorney reminded me of the words of Martin Luther King, Jr:

"The ultimate measure of a man is not where he stands in moments of comfort and convenience, but where he stands at times of challenge and controversy."

They also shared with me another profound statement by King, Jr:

"Injustice anywhere is a threat to justice everywhere."

I would like to thank my attorneys for believing in me and fighting for my freedom, Nuff love!!!

My family members, aunts, uncles, grandmother, parents, siblings, friends, and co-workers last and by no means least, my girlfriend, the one who has been a tower of strength through this ordeal.

A special thank you to the following persons; I have to make mention of you guys.

Phillip, Sharon, Selma, Lucas, Mr. P, Shaye, Dr. M.

Writing this book has been a new, yet challenging experience, an experience that has transformed my life. I have been somewhat humbled by the ordeal, learning to live within my means.

As you can see, I am continuing to live my life despite waiting on my case to return before the judge. I am walking and working in faith because faith without work is dead. I know when it is all said and done, God's promise will ring true. I will be exonerated, and I will live a blessed life. My story and my testimony will impact many lives. To God be all the glory.

A BIG THANK YOU TO YOU ALL

....

The End

Acknowledgement

Writing this book was a big challenge; however, I am compelled to tell the world about my ordeal. Firstly, I would like to thank Jehovah for the strength and sanity in bringing me through my trial so that I could put pen to paper to thank Him. Secondly, some special people made this piece of literature what it is today, a complete book, which I could not have done without the time, labour, and intellect of the following dedicated notable people.

My Immediate Family - I want to thank my parents and grandparents for their unrelenting love toward me. Their support before, during, and after the ordeal has strengthened my courage to overcome this devastating experience. Each visit when incarcerated meant so much to me. I am also grateful for the time and money spent because they knew I was innocent and held faith in me. I can never repay that kind of love shown, and I will never forget it even in a millennium.

Brothers, Aunts, Uncles, and In-laws - Thank you for all your financial and emotional support; you have my gratitude. I know I can never repay you guys, but I'll make you all proud one day.

My Girlfriend - I might not have known you before the incident, but you have been there for me through thick and thin, and for this, I am willing to spend the rest of my life with you.

Close Friends - You guys have been there for me no matter what, and your prayers have brought me through it all.

Note From Author

Black men are often falsely accused of crimes they have never committed. They are beaten, sentenced, abused, and their livelihood stripped away. This vicious act from days of slavery, rampant throughout the 1900s, lingers within society today and still occurs in modern-day Jamaica, despite development in crime-solving technology and the loud cries of injustice.

The criminal acts of abduction and robbery have changed me in ways sometimes unexplainable. I am confident that I would act differently if I were placed in a similar unfortunate situation. I would not be as trustworthy as I was then, in 2007, and before that. My fragile trust in humanity is one of the many areas I have changed. In the past, I was an individual who trusted people quickly without any questions asked. Sadly, many people in current society tend to take one's kindness for weakness.

I still do not allow that cruel experience to prevent new people from entering my life. Some of the kindest people I have met came into my life after the incident. I do not allow the actions of others to determine my decision to make meaningful relationships. I try my utmost best not to be judgemental in any way. As I, too, have been judged due to being incarcerated. As human beings, we are all prone to mistakes. However, the problem lies when we fail to learn from our mistakes.

Healing

On this topic of having healed from my ordeal, my answer to that question is I'm halfway there. The scars are there for life. Some are memories, no matter hard I try, cannot be erased; instead sometimes haunting. I've learned to use those terrible memories as stepping stones to overcome obstacles that I may encounter.

The Journey

Although the journey had me feeling bitter at one point, I learned an important lesson: nothing in life happens before the right time. Maybe God had a bigger purpose why my innocent victory was long in coming. All things in life work together for good for those who trust God.

The most important lesson I have learned throughout the traumatic journey is that we only live once. Therefore, we should try to live our lives to the fullest and live every day like our last! Life is indeed unpredictable. In all you do, do with a willing heart. You are never too old to learn or to say I'm sorry. Too often, we are wrong and try to justify such actions due to pride.

I am grateful for the opportunity to have lived through my ordeal; I could say, 13 years of my life were wasted. I am beyond asking why it happened to me, why I was the sacrificial lamb. What matters is that I survived it! I survived prison. I am still alive. Now, I have the chance to live life uninterrupted. Most importantly, I get the opportunity to tell the world about my experience, and I hope that my story motivates you to live life to its fullest!

Author's Contact

Email:
kirving@prescriptiontoprison.com

Facebook:
Prescription To Prison

Your Notes

Your Notes

Your Notes

Your Notes

KEVAUGHN IRVING